Morning Thoughts

become

Daily Things

By Denise L. Graves

edited by:

Mason Harrison and Ashanti George Paulin

MORNING THOUGHTS BECOME DAILY THINGS

Copyright © 2026 **Denise L. Graves**

ISBN (Paperback): 979-8-89672-262-5
ISBN (Ebook): 979-8-89672-263-2

5830 E 2nd St, Ste 7000 #9983
Casper, WY 82609
USA

Our lives are a reflection of our thoughts. Our thoughts represent what we truly believe and value. Our beliefs are foundational, informing and come from an assortment of places. If you want to change your life, change and shape your thoughts every morning. Everything else will follow.

Appreciation

Special thanks to Mildred L. Graves, my courageous mother who taught me that "Morning Thoughts become Daily Things." On my mother's clearest days, she would sing the song "I woke up this morning with my mind stayed on Jesus." For her Jesus was all that was good, healthy, loving, peaceful, providing and whole. That one word, Jesus, shaped what she could and would expect from the day. When I heard my mother singing, I knew my life would be better and certainly more peaceful. It is from her that I learned how "Morning Thoughts become Daily Things."

I appreciate my sisters who believed in me, my brothers who created distance for me to move around, my children, (Kaliff and Denisha, (children from other parents) Abiyah, Latisha, Thomas, Omar and Taylor) and all who have allowed me to nurture them. I thank all who entered my life to keep me growing, choosing to love and write — and the many people from all over the world who showed up as teachers, friends, colleagues, light workers, lovers and illusionary enemies.

Dedication to:

Jennifer Turner & the Community Book Center Family • Zion Hill Ministries Hope House of Kansas City, KS • Charlene, KU Professor, who advocated for me • Erma Cornelieus, Cousin/Aunt

Contents

Message from the author

Welcome to an amazing transformative moment. I have these moments often. Sometimes they do not feel pleasant. However, I know intellectually these moments are for my good. That is why I am writing this book. I want you to know that I am committed to my growth and your growth. I have learned that making decisions to change the quality of life is something we can all do.

I know this is possible because my life is different now. I grew up in a time when women were expected to be quiet and serve others no matter what the personal cost. Because I wanted to be loved, I did whatever I could to be considered indispensable, accepted and loved. I kept confidences not worthy of keeping, worked from sun up to sun down and I allowed others to trample all over my boundaries. That kind of behavior got me used, abused and discarded when someone or something better, more desirable, available or more indulging came along.

> I thought that being compliant and sweet is what it took to get what I wanted: love, respect, acceptance and abundance. I was wrong!

One day I took my mother's song to heart and woke up! With my innocence taken, body beaten and resources diminished, I decided that I wanted — NO — I deserved a better life. So, incrementally from the age of six, I began to declare the kind of life I wanted. I waged for space, respect and safety with my voice, thoughts and behaviors. Every day I woke up with my mind on better and good.

As I became more aware of my life's possibilities, I experimented with vocalizing my desire. I realized that as long as there was hope and a willingness to let go of thinking, speaking and doing things that were no longer giving or creating my good — my life would be better. That also included allowing people to leave or be a part of my life in adjusted roles on adjusted terms.

Something inside of me believed that I came from a place of hope and power. Yes, there were moments filled with complete despair. Unfortunately, bad things happen to little girls. People close to them do not hear their cries for help or they too, feel powerless. Sometimes these children take matters into their own hands. Sometimes these children are perceived as mean, mischievous or incorrigible. My moment of awakening happened at age six. So, in an effort to de-escalate my anger, after an episode of self-protection aggression, my mother held me upside down by the legs. It was her attempt to quite my voice of protest. In that moment with the top of my head facing the floor, I realized that my Morning Thoughts could become Daily Good Things. Here is part of my story:

I was seeded under conditions not desired by my mother or any respectable woman of that time. A man who knew not his greatness nor cared at the time put "something" in the drink of a woman out "on the town" with her friends. She remembers jumping out of the window of a motel room back into her painful life. Several weeks later, she learned she was pregnant with me.

I write this because something in my mother kept her going to raise eight children and keep the circumstances surrounding my conception a secret for more than 35 years. Her trauma produced bouts of anger, rage, self-hate, and bitterness directed toward me. It hurt both of us. Still, I loved her so. She was all I had. I wanted her to love me because I was good, lovable and existed.

My journey to wholeness was long. I was committed to the intense desire to create a loving, powerful, safe and peaceful life. The will to change always starts with a thought. I have learned that I can have what I think about all of the time. What I did not know was how long manifestation would take. So I kept the tradition alive in my family of waking up "with my mind stayed on Jesus — (all that is good)." I too, sang songs that refocused pain, aloneness and the sense of wandering in the wilderness.

Imagination is amazing. Imagine that all words are songs. Imagine what could happen if you woke up starting each day with words, feelings and hopes of what you want. I will share **Six Simple Ways** to assist you with creating thoughts that become good things.

As my mother learned to sing the old Negro Spiritual, "I woke up this morning with my mind stayed on Jesus," you can learn to wake up with your mind stayed on good, peace, healing, abundance, prosperity, possibilities and love.

This book is about how to intentionally create and allow thoughts that bring about our daily good no matter what. This book is for you of you ever found yourself thinking:

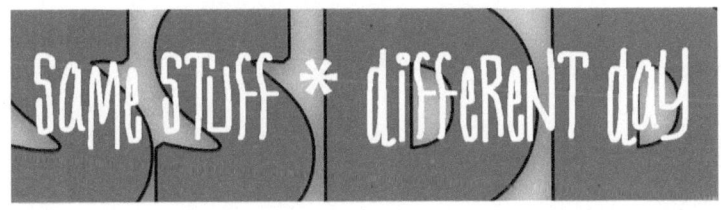

Step One —Think: It Gets Better

Every day you and I are changing.

Are you stuck and tired of not getting what you want? Do you find that some mornings it is harder to get out of bed because you dread the expected events of the day, the people you must work with or the places you need to go? If you answered "yes" to any of these, then this book is for you.

If you are ready for a change, then this is the book for you. You will learn how to start your day off  declaring and being open to receiving good things. This is your day to turn your life into something better. Actually, it is your time to co-create with the universe to produce an amazing life.

Everything happens in the mind. The old adage is true:

"As a person thinketh, so s/he is."

It will be hard to change the quality of your life if you cannot surrender to the possibility that your life can be better. One key to creating the desired change you want is to make room in your mind that other people are living healthier, wealthier and creative lives. Somewhere in the world there are people just like you enjoying immense good. They live in their ideal home, have vibrant health and have supportive and loving relationships. These people have enough money to pay bills, invest, share and give away. This could be you. All you have to do is change your thinking and expect your words to manifest.

Step One: Get up every morning and think:

Today is better than yesterday. It is the only day before me. I choose to say believe and know that.

Now say it! *Today is better than yesterday. It is the only day before me. I choose to say, believe and know that life gets better today because I am different. I have a made up mind to change. It gets better.*

That is the difference between you and those happy, peaceful and confident people: They wake up each day declaring and expecting their good. These same people are doing what they love, sleep restfully every night and enjoy environments that nourish their bodies, minds and spirits because they woke up one morning, and the next, **with their mind on what they wanted.**

This can be you!

Can you picture this truth — the place you are in right now is not the only place you will be forever? This place is not forever. This place is a stopover on your way to good. One thing for certain is change. Even in this moment your cells are different than when you began reading this passage. Time is marking its signature on your skin, hair, heart and mind without your permission. So give yourself a gift, learn how to wake up every morning declaring and living in happiness, health, wholeness and a sense of completeness.

Start right now and consider the words to this song by George Benson:

Everything must change
Nothing stays the same
Everything must change
No one stays the same

The young become the old
And mysteries do unfold
Cause that's the way of time
Nothing and no one goes unchanged

There are not many things in life
You can be sure of
Except rain comes from the clouds
Sun lights up the sky
And humming birds do fly

Winter turns to spring
A wounded heart will heal
But never much too soon
Yes everything must change

The young become the old
And mysteries do unfold
Cause that's the way of time
Nothing and no one goes unchanged

Benson is right, time moves on without our permission. The big question is: Do you want to be in this same place tomorrow? Do you want to be in this place new week? Do you want to be in this place a year, or 5 years from now? If your answer is no — speak change into your better life.

Remember another word for intention is hope.

What are you hoping for today?

Declare what you want with energy. It may sound silly at the beginning, but remember it happens in the spirit, mind and then matter (the physical). It gets better and so will you.

Change your movement signs from STOP to GO.

Thoughts......

_____
_____
_____
_____
_____
_____
_____
_____
_____
_____
_____
_____
_____
_____
_____
_____
_____
_____
_____
_____
_____

wake up with DETERMINATION. go to bed with SATISFACTION.

Step Two: One decision and one motion at a time

One New Year's eve my friend asked me to share my resolutions. I said, "I want my business to grow, make more money, be in love, travel the world and finish my books." I can still feel the chill that ran through my body that day because there is nothing like putting your hopes and dreams out into the universe. The second most important way to get to your desired place is to WAKE UP!

I was not always this clear. All I knew was that I did not want to be poor any more. I did not want people taking advantage of me. I did not want to be abused or abandoned.

What do you want? What do you not want?

These two questions require serious thought. Until you can develop an awareness of who you truly are and what you want — you will dread the day ahead, the people and upcoming activities. Your freedom is one conscious thought away. Will you decide to be free to live a full, abundant, loving and powerful life? Start by declaring "every day in every way I am getting better and better."

From infancy to about 20, most people are dumping sites for unsolicited data. We do not select our child care providers, elementary or often our high schools. We do not select our teachers or the material they share. We respond to their ideas, hopes, fears and dreams. Just think about it, as you read this book you are called to explore your basic foundational thoughts. Where did they come from and are those foundational thoughts true for your now?

BABY	YOUTH	TEEN	YOUNG ADULT	MATURE ADULT
Dependent	Compliant	Exploring	Sensing and experiencing	Power known

Even now, rarely do we consider what we authentically want. From the age of thirteen until we are in our mid-twenties, most of us struggle with the relevance, accuracy and appropriateness as well as the utility of that data imparted to us at early ages. Often while in the care of parents, teachers and tutors during that phase in our lives, we accept the data benefits — good and bad because they entitle us to some measure of freedom, joy, material acquisition and place.

However there comes a time, according to Gail

Sheehy, author of "Passages," and Daniel Levinson, author of "Seasons of a Man's Life," in which our "membership in culture (and society)" shifts.

Often we all experience transition hesitancy and believe we are not prepared or don't want to move to the next step. However, time passes and we are thrust into change often without our permission.

- As a **baby,** we absorb every form of stimulus exposed to us. We do not analyze it at all. We experience all of this with our eyes, ears, nose, taste, touch and internal genetic and spiritual sense.
- In our **youth** we move from unobjected observing and absorbing to the development of comparisons, questions, and compliance to assure optimum pleasure or freedom from harm. Sometimes this processes is augmented by exposure to diverse logic models to be explored later. The process is subtle and intentional by a multitude of sources competing for your life energy.
- During the end of the **teens** we sense that many of the earlier influences have meaning but we challenge if that meaning is in our best interest or fullest joy. It is important but we don't know why.

- In the **young adult stage** of the "Trying Twenties and Crisis Thirties" we realize that the benefits we once enjoyed do not bring joy, meaning and peace that it once did. In these places of transition and recognition is the place of power to authentically decide how we will act. These are our testing years.
- **Adulthood** is forever in a state of crystallization. Yes we are grown, yes we pay our bills, raise children, care for parents and more. But we also renegotiate the quality of life terms. Some of those decision include how we partner, what we really need to live comfortably, what adventures are on the horizon and more. Each of these life choice moments is where you redefine what it means to be uniquely you.

The moments of decision to change occurs throughout our lives. A time comes however, when you will know that something has to shift. This idea will come to you in many ways. Often trauma, crisis or attainment of a goal is the catalyst for change. When that moment presents itself don't just respond, Act. Power is really the ability to act. The first action to change happens in our emotions and then our conscious mind. As you build wisdom and embrace learning through experiences, you become more mindful and your actions are more intentional. You are more confident and hopefully more compassionate with self and those on the change journey with you.

When we embrace the sweet taste of better, there is the temptation to desire what I did that one New Year's Eve: to do and have everything all at once. I did not know how to take one step at a time to build what I wanted. I learned that my desired outcomes of money, good job, nice house, good care, love, peace and travel required respectful thought, research, movement and timing. Keep in mind that one good thought begets another. Each new thought builds upon the other. Start declaring that you want something better. Sit with this for a moment. What does better look like for you?

Step 2: Practice one desired behavior for 21 days without interruption. If you miss a day start the process all over again. Scientists have proven that any behavior repeated with intention and without interruption is incorporated into our daily lives. Start with one thing at a time.

Think: Every day in every way I am getting better.

When I seriously considered what I wanted that year that would put me in a place of power, high energy and tangible products I had to do some things differently. The first decision was to declare that something better is possible for me. I was not uniquely alone. Every great leader, parent, teacher, student, dancer, business owner, performer and athlete made a conscious decision to change. Have you ever wondered why that thing you want most is not coming to you? Take a moment and check yourself. When did you declare you wanted something more but never changed what you were doing to get it? The old adage is true: ***Insanity is doing the same things you have always done but expecting different results.***

Take for example my preparation for math tests. I had an ability to know the right answers to math questions. I did not know how to explain the process or show how I got the answers. So when I took tests and could not demonstrate the process, I received a poor test score for not demonstrating the problem solution logic model. As long as I prepared the same way for the test, the results were the same — a negative grade. When I changed my test preparation process, the grade outcomes changed. I worked tediously to answer one problem at a time. I set aside time every day to allow myself to develop a new skill. I took the time to display my mental processing to arrive at the solution on paper, it was only then that I received better grades. Heck, I eventually became an algebra tutor.

Here is what I have learned, anyone who wants something different must do something different. It is not a matter of "I want this, but not that," but not changing. It is a matter of discerning what you really want. The hard part is honestly identifying and owning what you want because there are many distractions. Most of us want something better and different, but we do not really know what better would look like. So we borrow the better of other people. Take for example, our desire to be healthy. We want to be healthy but we have no idea of what healthy looks like so we mimic some television personality, rock star or athlete, etc. We buy what we see them wear. Walk like they walk; talk like they talk; and/or do what we see them do.

Without exploration of how these people chose to pay attention to the smallest details of their lives, we end up living the life of a parrot — copying what we see and hear.

Take a minute and imagine your life better tomorrow than it is today.

What would be different?

What do you need to change to produce a different outcome?

How long do you want the outcome to endure?

When this behavior changes how will you think and relate to your new aspect of the self?

Make a list of what you want. Once you have listed what you want, prioritize what you want. Pick one item to work on first then select a small thought, words, behavior or activity to change. If the item selected to change is too drastic, any crisis could take you back to square one. Do small things first, add a new thing as you are ready? Select something and stick to it. It is an illusion that the most successful people are those who multi-task, work faster, longer and more deeply all of the time. Choosing to change one thing at a time creates the mental, emotional, physical and spiritual space to embrace the change. Often there are other benefits to this decision including efficiency and mental clarity. This is the time you can honestly assess where you are in the moment, where you want to go and what it will take to get you there. In this moment of discernment you will find your place of power. Give it its good time and make the decision.

A note of caution — abrupt changes produce a return to a comfortable bad behavior whenever a crisis occurs. Start slowly, one moment, hour and day at a time. You can do it. Declare this truth and start your thought, word and behavior change today.

Every day in every way, I am getting better and better.

Thoughts......

Step Three: Practize, Practise, Practice

Practice means to perform, over and over again in the face of all obstacles, some act of vision, of faith, of desire. Practice is a means of inviting the perfection desired. —**Martha Graham**

"The only limits in my life are the limits I place on myself."

—*Denise L. Graves*

One of my friends said, "Anyone can be great at something if they practice it 1,000 times." Over the years I have given considerable thought to this statement and looked for holes in it. I am curious as to why I would want to dispel some idea that could bring me to a place of better. I recently accepted that I thought that way because I could not envision me being greater than that moment. Some old tape was running around in my head unchecked. That tape was relaying someone else's limitation.

I decided that I had outgrown other people's limitations - so I wrote down what I wanted on an index card. And on a small piece of paper, I wrote them again. I stuffed it into my pocket. I walked around with my new hopes and dreams and sat by the river. While watching the sunrise and sunset I pulled out the paper and looked at it. I was conditioning my mind to accept something different little by little. I practiced the idea of better so that I could focus on and hope for something different. For a while it was my little secret.

Pretty soon, I became so occupied with my hopes and dreams, I started reading my desires out loud. When asked what I wanted in life, without thinking I said what I had been reading from my small pieces of paper. I began to believe my hopes and dreams. I thought about it day and night. Every behavior was judged by what I had written on those pieces of paper. I had learned the value of practice.

Good ideas are not adopted automatically. They must be driven into practice with courageous patience.

—Hyman Rickover

During my 20 year career as a faith based organizer, we used a principal essential in honoring the human potential — voice power. The principal, "the first revolution is internal," reminds me that when I am ready to change, I must first change my thoughts, words and behaviors. You must go inside to listen to the tapes running around unchecked. Take a look at your basic behavior patterns. Explore why you do what you do and say what you say. Listen to how you speak to yourself and others. Go inside. Most of us try to convince others that we are great and powerful. The weakness with that work is that acting for many of us is easy to do — it is also exhausting. Internal alignment with our good starts with our ability to decide on what we want, say it, write it down, act on it and celebrate when it is done.

You and I are changing in every way for the good each day. We do not have to convince anyone of this truth. We have to allow ourselves to uncover this idea of internal revolution. Our daily declaration of who we are, what we want and how we will get there counters every obstacle in ourselves that is contrary to where we want to go.

Practicing the new truth about yourself as the first thoughts in the morning will set the tone for the each day for the rest of your life. Just as you practiced walking, talking and anything else you wanted to accomplish — you must practice now.

"Do you remember the 21 day rule which states that any behavior, word or thought practiced for 21 days without interruption will become a part of your better life routine." If for any reason the new routine is interrupted before the 21st day — start all over again.

To achieve what you want in life — it is important to practice thinking, talking and doing what you want — right now. The decision is yours. As you set your course for change, repetition will be a big part of it. Repetition will plant new and better thoughts, cancel out untrue messages and quiet the voices of anyone in the way of our greatest good. Today, before you go to bed declare — *Every day in every way I am getting better and better.* Continue to give your mind other things to focus on. When you wake up feeling unhappy, tired, dreading the day or uncertain that the new day will be any different or better than the day before — intentionally create space in your mind for a better thought. Think about something or someone you truly enjoy. Allow yourself to smile. Now think about having your good — declare for no reason the following:

I declare peace, abundance, health and success in my life today!
I declare peace, abundance, health and success in my life today!
I declare peace, abundance, health and
success in my life today!

Thoughts......

_____
_____
_____
_____
_____
_____
_____
_____
_____
_____
_____
_____
_____
_____
_____
_____
_____
_____
_____
_____
_____
_____
_____
_____

The more you praise and celebrate your life, the more there is in life to celebrate.
—Oprah Winfrey

Step Four: Praise yourself

You done good — go ahead and say it. Every time you practice your morning phrases, celebrate yourself. Give in to the glorious joy of changing. Look in the mirror and smile while telling yourself "you done good" or something respectfully similar.

Let us get this out of the way. Yes, it is important to compliment and praise yourself. To do this is not being egocentric, it is not being prideful and does not demonstrate a lack of humility. What self-praise does is remove our dependence on others to define us. We intrinsically know when we have completed a task, accomplished a feat and overcome an obstacle. What happens when we do not recognize our power to affirm ourselves we invalidate our word and worth to ourselves. We put ourselves in the position of needing a traveling fan club. And often sustaining a traveling fan club robs us of our ability to be ourselves. When we need other people to give us value by complimenting, praising or "attaboy, atta-girl," we set ourselves up to being a slave to the opinion of others. When you can own your measurement standards and applaud completion, growth, success, better and new — you are living in authenticity.

Yes many sages speak against high mindedness, hypocrisy, self-adulation, and self-aggrandizement. These are extremes. They are unrelated to the acknowledgment of task completion and climbing the ladder to ascension and success. Never let another's word about you be more powerful than the word you tell to yourself. Work to never tell yourself a lie about yourself. Do not hide in the untruth.

Sometimes we don't change because we are afraid of what other people will think or we worry about how we will look in the change process. I admit that sometimes change looks messy. But get this, you cannot live your life for anyone but yourself. Because people will come and go. People will change. At the end of the day — you are your constant. Lovers will come, change and sometimes go, children will grow-up and leave, parents will be immersed in their own concerns (or should be), colleagues/school mates/friends will change. You want to be tuned into the value of your own voice. You want to know its weight and worth is far beyond measure. Because this is the voice that matters in time and eternity. Any message you received that is contrary to supporting and honoring your good and respecting your voice is no longer necessary.

There was a poem written by Edgar Albert Guest called *Myself.*

I have to live with myself and so,
I want to be fit for myself to know
I want to be able as days go by
Always to look myself straight in the eye
I don't want to stand with the setting sun
And hate myself for the things I have done.

I don't want to keep on a closet shelf
A Lot of secrets about my self
And fool myself as I come and go
In to thinking no one else will ever know
The kind of person I really am.

I don't want to dress up myself in sham.
I want to go with my head erect
I want to deserve all men's' respect;
But here in the struggle for fame and wealth
I want to be able to like myself.

I don't want to look at myself and know that
I am bluster and bluff and empty show
I never can hide myself from me;
I see what others may never see;
I know what others may never know
I never can fool myself and so

Whatever happens I want to be
Self-respecting and conscience free.

You can get to know yourself better by applauding every effort you make to become your best self. I coach people to success because I believe in the good they are working to uncover. I believe that every word matters. I believe that the first words spoken in the morning about you matters. Dietitians state that the first food eaten in the day sets the tone for how you will think, speak and act. For example, if you eat something sweet the first thing in the morning, chances are you will want sweets throughout the day. So imagine what would happen if you spoke the truth about who you are becoming every day — eventually your mind and body will believe what you say.

It seems like the Burger King® marketing team put a corner on the market with the slogan "have it your way!" Well, if you check many ancient texts and words of wise sages and crones, you will find message after message regarding the power of the spoken word. The Hebrew Scripture reminds us to ask and it shall be given and that we have not because we ask not. So what do you have to lose? Declare you're good. Affirm it is happening.

Move into the direction of your good and celebrate every little step. You done good!!!

Consider writing your own manifesting affirmations. Some possible active word sentences could begin like the following:

I am prosperous
I know my good is at hand
I love my vital health
I have all my needs provided for this day.

Be creative declare what you want. Test the process. Don't try to tell the universe how to do it. Let the "how to" details unfold. The power of your energized and sincere word is always acted upon.

Thoughts......

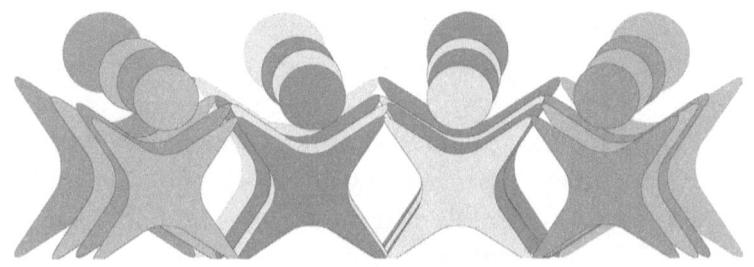

Step Five: Build a Team

All stories about sheroes and heroes who save the day include some obscure person that believes in him or her. Think about it. In the cartoons or movies when Superman is at his lowest, the camera spans the community to find some person uttering words of support and hope. In the old movies, it was the redheaded photographer Jimmy Olsen or the awestruck reporter, Lois Lane. In the mythology of powerful women, it was Wonder Woman. Her supporter was Etta Candy.

It seems that every sacred faith community has stories used often to demonstrate powerful leadership with supporting casts. Moses in the Torah, the adopted son of Pharaoh's daughter was considered a superhero. His team members were Pharoah's daugther; brother, Aaron; sister, Miriam and father-in-law, Jethro.

In *The Matrix* movie series, the hero, Neo, benefited from the undying support of Morpheus, the wisdom of the Oracle, computer skills, and love of Trinity. Leaders create support teams. Leaders walk into their life assignment often with trepidation and unexplained faith. Most recently, cartoon leaders like *Dora the Explorer,* has Boots. You get my point? The role of the sidekick is to support, be a mirror, challenge, provide a voice of reason, and really get to see the real you. They love you, are loyal, look for you if you disappear and hold their ground to keep you from failing or falling hard.

No one is an island. In the movie, *Cloud Atlas,* the stars Halle Berry and Tom Hanks represent characters whose many lives have one singular assignment — live a creative free full life of love. In each lifetime the one phrase that connects all major characters is "Our lives are not our own. We are bound together by our past, present and future." As you build your team remember that everyone you encounter now is a partner in your legacy pool. Each of us has the opportunity to assemble a team to help us fulfill our "Souls Assignment." In this book authored by Rev. Chis Michael, we are reminded that each of us are on the earth to do something specific. Every experience in your life moves you in the direction of your life assignment. As you explore your life, what circumstances, types of people, joys and pains keep showing up. As you work to uncover what you are here to do, think about how your past, present and future are linked. Pay attention to connected streams, themes, or conditions.

What kind of person or persons do you need to be your greatest self? Who will invest in you enough to make sure your assigned tasks are completed? When we make the decision to make our lives better, we are conspiring with the universe to manifest the best outcome.

I am a movie buff. The movie *Akeelah and the Bee,* is a story where one girls' dream is supported by a teacher, tutor, her wayward brother, postal worker and more. Once people see you are moving toward your goal, you too will have over 5,000 coaches. There are scenes in the movie when everyone she encounters says something or does something to move her to her goal. Who are your supporters, naysayers and observers? Who do you want to help you get to your next step, your next level of growth?

Think about building an intentional team. When this team is in place, they bring you to the place where you are fully present, better, expanded and impactingly powerful. No one is an island no matter how much we think we live a hermit's life. We are interdependent with each other — from the food we eat, the air we breathe and the water we use. Our opportunity is to facilitate an ample gathering of a team or "on assignment" souls so that everyone is in the process of fulfilling their divine destiny.

Some things to consider when building a personal Effectiveness Team

1. Create a clear Intention of what you want to do.
2. Select 4 to 5 people to act as a group that supports your growth and is self-conscious about their own life operations, the change process, and they are willing and able to create rules of engagement.
3. Clearly set intentions, goals and allow the team to help celebrate small accomplishments.
4. Meet regularly and check-in frequently for a period of 3-5 months.
5. Keep track of the journey. Create a time line or vision board.
6. Allow and help your team feel free to express their feelings as well as their ideas. Disagreement will occur. View this as healthy and good.
7. Encourage each individual to carry their own weight.
8. Support an atmosphere of honest critique that is frequent, frank and spoken with grace and love.
9. Allow leadership of the group to shift from time to time.

Sources: The Human Side of Enterprise, by Douglas MacGregor;
The Wisdom of Teams, by Kaztenbach and Smith
(Modified by Peace Ministry LLC 2014)

Many of us cannot image convening a group to take a look at our lives. Often we want an easy way to move into a desired change so we try to do it alone. It is possible to do it alone. But, it is more fun however to have cheer leaders along the way. It is no accident that you are reading this book and contemplating what to do now in your life. You are on purpose and in the right time. I have learned much more about right action and divine timing while allowing myself to be coached and coaching others. The old adage that states "When the student is ready. The teacher shows up," is about divine timing.

The teacher has been trained specifically for the developmental needs of the student.

I want to be your coach because it has been ordained by something larger than ourselves. We will learn and grow in ways we cannot imagine. Our collective responsibility is to be open to possibilities. Will you dare to dream and work for your better life? I will, if you will; and I will be ready when you are ready.

It is important to identify several people who will support your decision to change, intentional success messaging and behaviors to do something better and different. I do not recommend telling your plan to everyone, but you can begin to gravitate toward people who invest in you so that you can invest in your goals and dreams. All enlightened leaders have followers, informants and supporters.

Thoughts......

Step Six: Add Another Activity

Life is about constant change. Even when you are intentional about one thing other opportunities, resources and ideas show up. Day turns into night, seasons change, cells die and while your hair grows or falls out you begin to shine.

Your moment of opportunity is now. Now that you have made the decision to build a better life by starting your day with thoughts, words and behaviors to manifest your good — keep moving forward. It's time to decide what to say next to inform your continuous re-thinking life. For starters commit to a phrase that I acquired from great motivators.

Every day in every way I am getting better and better. Every day my better is being revealed to me. Today my better is.....

Once I decided to love myself totally and unconditionally, I had to learn what this kind of love looked like on me. So keep in mind that when what you want is so different than what you have ever had, breathe. Look inside, examine your request and ask the question "What is this?" The answer you find will open up another opportunity to create. When I accepted the gift of loving myself, the revelation of the look of love as beautiful, strong and healing caused me to reduce negative self-talk, stop accepting disrespect, living small and more. Simple intentional morning thoughts and words shaped how I looked at everything in my life.

You too, can find this amazing power within your thoughts, words and behaviors. The liberation from low self-worth, damaging pessimism and death produces energy, attracts prosperity, peace, harmony, needed resources and so much more.

Create a plan for change and put it on a realistic time line. Act in discipline. Practice, share and practice some more. Treat your own growth as a corporate visioning and strategic plan. Invest in yourself and enjoy the dividends.

So, try to take your time in making changes in your life. Also, give yourself permission to give good attention to one major life adjustment at a time. Often our weakness is that we get caught in the confusion of trying to do all things at once.

The value of supportive change is reflection. Slowing our mind down enough to recognize the impact of new decisions and behaviors on your life and the people and places around you.

Do not give up the new behaviors acquired during this process. As you let go of thoughts no longer appropriate for your now, you will have space for better and better. Practice your new thoughts, words and behaviors as you go to the next life healing activity.

Thoughts......

Summary

'To create the change you want you must be willing to change your thoughts, words and behaviors. As an evolving adult you have the opportunity to reconstruct how you spend each 24 hours. These simple 6 steps will assist you on your journey to becoming your best self. Your intentionality makes all the difference in the world.

Think on these things:

- **Know that without a doubt that — It gets better**

Believe in the possibility of good and that you deserve that good all of the time.

- **Do one decision and motion at a time**

Multi-tasking may be the order of the day but it cannot allow you to know your own mind. Consider giving yourself the privilege of working toward change slowly one step at a time.

- **Practice, Practise, Practize**

A persons habits tell who they are. You create healthy habits by creating disciplines for success through practice. Use the 10,000 hour rule — anything you practice becomes a habit. Your habits tells everyone who you really are.

- **Praise yourself**

Self-applause for reaching specific benchmark is important. Turn your voice of criticism and doubt into appreciation and celebration. Life is a journey, not a destination. So recognize your own good, growth, meaning and accomplishments.

- **Build a team**

There is a story about the formation in which geese, fly. I like it because they alternate gaggle leadership. When the leader gets tired, it moves in the ranks and another leaders emerges. If one of them is injured, it leaves the formation and several geese accompany the other to safety. When we select a team to support us, we give ourselves permission to be a part of the "wing span" and be carried by the steam of others. When this occurs we do not become overly tired or overwhelmed. We are buoyed by the cushion of others. Keep in mind that your direction is always your choice and when it is time you will forsake any direction that does not honor your dream. You will find that your supports will take a pause from their direction to fly with you. Build a conscious team.

- **Add another activity**

There are two major types of thinkers: field and sequence. When we multi-task we are employing the experience of a field thinker-juggling multiple thoughts, words and activities. This practice serves a good purpose in the short run of change work. It allows many influences to converge in one direction allowing "a change pin point." It is labor and energy expensive. It requires constant redirect. The second type of thinker is sequential. This thinker lives in the logic model of order and priorities. This thinker often does one activity at a time. When the activity is done, then they move one. Its benefit is that it is easier to experience benchmark completion. It allows for reflection, evaluation and planning.

Give yourself time to reap the benefits that include the lessons learned from intentional change.

NOTE: You will experience re– sistance or **pushback** in this process. This is normal. It often protects us from impulsive actions that counters our safety. However, it is important to push through barriers that block us from our good. Consider giving your selfpermission to release and old thought, word or behavior to allow for your greater good. The affirming "permissioning" statement could look something like this:

"I release this thought, word and/or behavior. It has served me well. It is no longer needed for my new life vision. Thank you for all the ways it benefited me in the past. I release you to my highest and greatest good. I now live in my most present right moment. For this is my place of power."

Note that life is about balance and support. Many people fizzle out just before the desired outcome is experienced. Don't give up. Stay the course. Meditate, play, pray, dance, sing, love and more. You are worthy of all the good. The ball is as they in tennis, is in your court.

What will you do?

Well, for now this concludes this brief discussion on how **Morning Thoughts become Daily Things** by employing these **"6 Simple Steps."**

One technique that has worked for me and some of my clients is the creation of an affirmation calendar. At one setting, I put the following affirmations in my calendar. This was my first step of establishing a new disciple — planned positive affirmations. My next step was to repeat each affirmation a minimum of 7 times in the morning. It was a little tedious at first. However, I noticed that how I experienced my day was more positive, peaceful and I just felt good. It also encouraged me to tune out anything that was contrary to my intent.

Things began to shift my appearance improved, attitude was more optimistic, my words lovingly truthful and I began to attract amazing good.

For more support, find a life coach like myself and secure the kind of life you really want to live by changing your Morning Thoughts.

Thoughts......

Affirmations

Every day in every way I am getting better and better.	Right now I am getter better and better.	It was a good day. I did the best I knew to do.	Today, my level of authentic engagement increase with myself.
I love myself totally and uncon– ditionally as I am right now	I am confidently growing and I am at peace with this.	I am healthy whole and complete.	My health is divinely given and earthly appreciated.
My life looks like my choices. Today I choose my better.	Right now I am choosing only the best for me.	Today I made good choices and now I let go of the worries of the day.	I surrender to the guidance of the creator and am open to receive only good.
Every day in every way I am getting better and better	I attract the right and perfect people in my life today	I release the worries of this day	Right now I am enough for every occasion.

Today is better than yesterday.	Every day in every way I am getting better and better	My good comes to me easily and effortlessly	I breathe easily and effortlessly in divine provision.
I see myself through the eyes of love	I am confident that things are working for my good.	Every day in every way I am getting better and better	I allow wisdom to teach me and courage to help me act wisely.
I declare peace, abundance, health and success in my life today!	I am open to intentional change.	My thoughts become things. I thinking on only what I want.	I accept my divine manifesta – tion of good all day long.

The key to changing old thoughts and replacing them with new thoughts is attention, planning for success and repetition. Say each affirmation 21 times each time. Try doing this in the mirror and see what happens.

Saying what you want allows you to trust your own voice. As you trust your own voice, you will begin to really accept your possibilities. This repetition provides a better thinking rhythm.

Another option is to put these affirmations on your calendar and do for 28 days. You will be surprised with the results.

Why Peace Ministry?

Healing the world requires all souls to be on assignment. Often it is difficult to learn our true purpose because there are so many intruders and assaults to the human body, spirit and mind. The treadmill we find ourselves on blocks each of us from knowing our worth.

Peace is the way I choose to live this life. Waging peace is about clarity, change, persistence, partners, evolving and learning through trial and error over and over again.

The individual, family unit, community and the world must seed into the righteous development, correction and rebirth of our good. I am committed to that. I invite you to be the power of love, peace, growth and birth through change. I know you are the partner I and others need to "do peace service."

My definition of Peace is "enoughness." Enough good food, housing, resources, provisions, harmony, abundance, love, respect, meaning, clean air, health, recreation, joy and safety for everyone on the planet. It is the full well-being and pursuit thereof as described in the Hebrew word "Shalom."

As an individual, parent, member of a family, friend, business owner, and community worker, with experience in numerous industries, I have learned that everyone benefits from a support network. However, each of us chooses how our surrounding network affirms our humanity and concept of divinity. When we find that we want a deeper and fuller experience, we work toward it. We choose to be more than before.

Our choices inform our growth, effectiveness, success and life assignment succession. Peace Ministry provides resources that come from expansive alternative wellbeing methodologies that have proven to enhance the quality of many lives. Working with you is my desire.

At the end of the day I want my "well-being" partner to know this:

- You are surrounded by a host of supporters who want only your good.
- You are in a safe place to show up and examine your life.
- You have the power and right to redefine your life at will.
- I am well equipped and resourced to help you get to your best good for your now."

*Note: If this is not true for you then it is certainly time to change your mind and attract supportive people.

Peace Ministry Services

Spiritual Advisor and Counseling
Life Coaching
Motivational Speaker
Relationship/Family Mediator
Wedding and other Ceremonies' Officiate

In Memory:
Mildred Louise Graves, my mother;
Rueben and Barbara Reid
Leif Browne and Frankie Lawson Brother Israel Hawkins Sr.

Morning Thoughts become Daily Things

Peace Ministry LLC and Institute, building
relationships that heal and enhance our World
peaceministry77@gmail.com
peaceministry2day.com
913.221.7212 Messages

PEACE MINISTRY, LLC

Writing things down makes them real.

My legacy unfolds with each step I take.

I author my own story.

The place of power is in the present.

"I Am" is always your core.

The only person you can change is you.